D0004891

History and Activities of the
Islamic Empire

Gary E. Barr

Heinemann Library
Chicago, Illinois

Customer Service 888-454-2279
Visit our website at www.heinemannlibrary.com

Designed by Kimberly R. Miracle in collaboration with Cavedweller Studio
Originated by Chroma Graphics
Printed in China by WKT Company Limited

11 10 09 08 07
10 9 8 7 6 5 4 3 2 1

The Library of Congress has cataloged the first edition as follows:
Barr, Gary, 1951-
        History and activities of the Islamic Empire / Gary E. Barr.-- 1st ed.
              p. cm. -- (Hands-on ancient history)
        Includes bibliographical references and index.
        ISBN 1-4034-7926-7 (HC) -- ISBN 1-4034-7934-8 (PB)
        1. Islamic Empire--Juvenile literature. I. Title. II. Series.

DS38.3.B37 2006
909'.09767--dc22   2005035170
13-digit ISBNs:
978-1-4034-7926-6 (hardcover)
978-1-4034-7934-1 (paperback)

Acknowledgments
The author and publishers are grateful to the following for permission to reproduce photographs: Alamy Images, p. 4 (Jon Bower); Art Directors and Trip. pp. 8 (Private Collection), **16** (Helene Rogers); Bridgeman Art Library, pp. 7 (Bibliotheque Nationale, Paris, France), **9**, **12** (Bibliotheque Nationale, Paris, France, Archives Charmet), **14** (The Trustees of the Chester Beatty Library, Dublin), **15** (Bibliotheque Nationale, Paris, France), **18** (Institute of Oriental Studies, St. Petersburg, Russia, Giraudon), **20** (Kairouan, Tunisia), **21** (Louvre, Paris, France, Peter Willi), **26** (Royal Asiatic Society, London, UK); Corbis, pp. **10** (Thomas Hartwell), **11** (Steve Raymer), **13** (Adam Woolfitt); Bridgeman Art Library/Private Collection, p. 4 book illustration by Munro Scott Orr (b. 1874) from World's Fairy Tale Book pub. By G. Harrap & Co. Ltd., London; Eye Ubiquitous, p. **17** (Hutchison); Harcourt, pp. **19** (David Rigg), **25** (David Rigg), **29** (David Rigg).

Front cover image of a Persian brass bowl reproduced with permssion of Art Resource, NY/Victoria & Albert Museum, London. Back cover image of a mosque reproduced with permission of Getty Images/Photodisc.

The publishers would like to thank Fred Donner and Eric Utech for their assistance in the preparation of this book.

Every effort has been made to contact copyright holders of any material reproduced in this book. Any omissions will be rectified in subsequent printings if notice is given to the publisher.

Table of Contents

Some words are shown in bold, **like this.** You can find out what they mean by looking in the glossary.

Chapter 1: Empire on Three Continents

Between about 600 and 1100 c.e., the Islamic Empire controlled large parts of Asia, Africa, and Europe. The empire had a powerful government and army. Its merchants traded goods with people far away. It was one of the world's most advanced civilizations. There were craftspeople, doctors, scientists, musicians, and artists.

The leaders of the Islamic Empire followed the religion of Islam. A person who follows Islam is called a **Muslim**. The central teachings of Islam are contained in the **Koran**. This is Islam's holy book. Muslims believe that the Koran contains the words of God. These words were revealed to their prophet, Muhammad. The Koran teaches that there is only one God. It says that every person must recognize God and follow the laws of Islam.

Muhammad was born in Mecca, in what is now Saudi Arabia. He began to teach his religious ideas there. Mecca became Islam's most holy city. Later, Muhammad moved to Medina. He founded a Muslim community there.

Timeline

Around 570	632	634–644	661	711-714
Muhammad is born.	Muhammad dies, the first caliph is selected to rule.	Believers movement takes over Syria, Iraq, Persia, and Egypt.	Damascus, Syria, becomes capital city of the Islamic Empire.	Muslims conquer Spain.

At first, Muhammad's followers were called Believers. Muhammad wanted them to start a society that recognized one God. The Believers wanted to spread these ideas beyond Arabia. But Muhammad died in 632 C.E. before this could happen.

Muslims pray in a mosque. Mosques often took on the architectural characteristics of the areas they were in.

750	900–1100	1096	1206	1258
Abbasids take control of Islamic Empire.	Unified Islamic Empire under the Abbasids gradually breaks into smaller Muslim states.	The Crusades from Europe to **Middle East** begin.	Muslims gain control of a large portion of India.	Mongol invaders capture Baghdad. The last Abbasid caliph is killed.

Caliphs

After Muhammad died, his followers chose a new leader. This leader was called a caliph. Caliphs were religious leaders as well as political leaders. The first caliphs raised armies. They sent the armies to other countries to spread Muhammad's teachings. By 680 the Believers had defeated several other empires. They took over land in Iraq, Iran, Syria, and parts of North Africa. By 750, the caliphs ruled an area that stretched from Spain to the Indus River in Pakistan.

When the Believers came to new countries, most of the people they met were Christians or Jews. The Believers let them keep their own religion, but they had to pay taxes to the caliph. They also had to live by the laws of Islam. Some Christians and Jews joined the Believers.

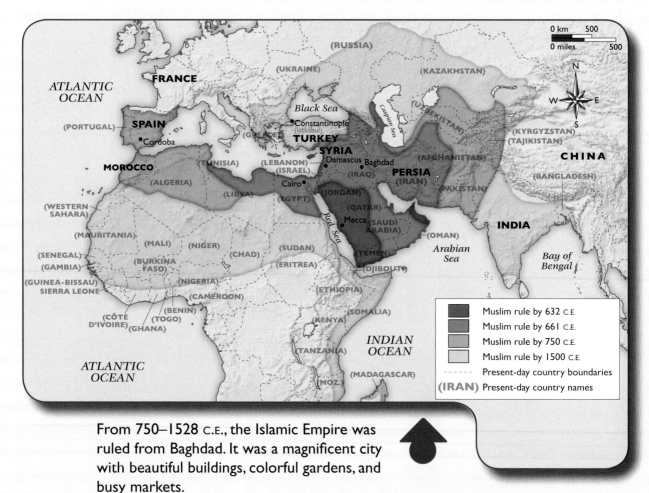

From 750–1528 C.E., the Islamic Empire was ruled from Baghdad. It was a magnificent city with beautiful buildings, colorful gardens, and busy markets.

Enemies attacked the Islamic Empire many times in its last years of existence. Baghdad fell to Mongol invaders in 1258 C.E.

Later, the caliphs decided that only those who followed the **Koran** were true Believers. These people were called **Muslims**. From then on, Islam became more separate from other religions.

The Golden Age

The very first caliphs ruled from Medina. The capital soon moved to Damascus, Syria. At this time, the caliphs belonged to the Umayyad family. In 750 another family, the Abbasids, took over. They soon built a new capital at Baghdad in Iraq. The empire was at its most powerful from 750 to about 1050 C.E. The Abbasid family was in power then. It is considered the Golden Age of the Islamic Empire.

The Abbasids ruled until 1258. However, after about 950 they became less powerful. The Islamic Empire broke into several smaller states. Many of the smaller states still saw the caliph as their religious leader. Spain, Egypt, Yemen, and several parts of Iran became independent. In 1258, the Mongols from Central Asia captured Baghdad and killed the last caliph.

The Golden Age was an exciting time. Goods from Asia, Africa, and Europe were traded in the Islamic Empire. Merchants sold high-quality steel, beautiful fabrics, and many other valuable items. They also introduced new payment methods. Baghdad and other cities of the empire became rich. They had beautiful hospitals, libraries, palaces, and public gardens.

Muslim scholars studied ideas from India, Egypt, and other places. They also studied the work of ancient Greeks. Soon Muslim scholars made their own contributions. For example, mathematicians made many discoveries. One type of mathematics now has an Arabic name: algebra. Muslim scientists invented new tools and equipment. Some types, such as beakers, are still used today.

By the 700s C.E. there were a number of great scientists and mathematicians in the Islamic Empire.

Muslim doctors developed many new medical techniques. They wrote down their discoveries in a huge encyclopedia. The book suggested treatments for most illnesses and injuries. Muslim medical books were translated into other languages. They used in Europe until the 1600s.

Muslim scientists calculated the shape and size of the earth. They did this long before Europeans did. Muslim scientists also invented the astrolabe. This useful tool helped travelers find their way. Explorers such as Christopher Columbus often studied Muslim books. They learned from the achievements of Muslim scholars.

A good story

Writers were highly respected in the Islamic Empire. "A Thousand and One Nights" was a collection of stories. The stories told about the empire's many different lands, as well as other places. "Aladdin and His Magic Lamp" was one of the stories. It is still one of the world's most popular tales today.

Aladdin uses his magic carpet to fly to a new adventure in a far-off place.

Desert life

The **Middle East** has many different environments. Some parts are desert and some parts have plenty of water. Some parts of the Middle East contain mountains that get cold and snow in the winter. In the desert, the environment affected the way people built houses. Because there were few trees, there was little wood to build homes. People built homes of dried mud covered by a protective coating. The flat roofs of the homes provided a cool place to sleep and eat. The lower floor was used for cooking, storage, and sometimes as a shelter for animals.

The houses of rich people were built around beautiful courtyards. These courtyards often had a fountain surrounded by flowers and tropical plants. Inside the houses were brightly-colored carpets, seat cushions, and elegant brass candlesticks.

An oasis is a place with water even though it is in a desert. They form when underground water comes to the surface or when rivers flow through such a place.

Islam has strict beliefs that a woman's beauty should only be seen by family members. Even women wearing modern fashions should dress modestly in public.

Desert clothing was loose fitting and light to keep people as cool as possible. Both men and women wore long-sleeved robes. This protected their skin from the sun. Strict religious law required Islamic women to cover their hair, and sometimes their face.

Food

In areas conquered by the empire, people continued to eat traditional foods. Islamic law and Middle Eastern spices influenced their cooking. In desert areas lamb was the main meat for meals. Several types of vegetables and breads were also served. Herbs, spices, and onions added extra flavor. Fruits, cakes, and pastries were common desserts. People drank camel, goat, or cow's milk. Milk was often turned into yogurt or cheese. Coffee, tea, and fruit juices were also popular drinks.

Muslim families were known for being very close. Many family members lived in the same house. The father was the leader. He listened to others, but made the important decisions. Families took good care of all the members. When a woman married, she went to live with her husband's family. Sons sometimes stayed with their own family after marriage. Women had less freedom and power in public life.

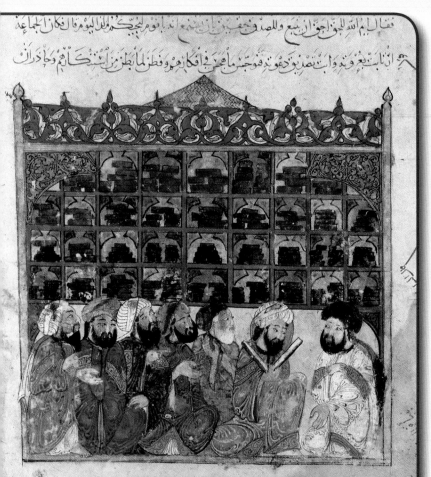

Schools

Some villages and towns had a school. This was where village children learned to read, write, do math, and read the **Koran**. They used slate tablets to write lessons. Further studies took place in schools located in mosques. Poor children did not always attend school. Younger children were taught about Islam by learning the Koran. This was very important. Islam was considered a way of living, not just a religious belief.

Most students started training for jobs when they were twelve.

Schools in the Islamic Empire were not just for children. Scholars often shared knowledge with each other.

A few of the best students took other subjects. They might become teachers, doctors, or other important leaders. Very few girls went to school past the age of twelve. They were expected to stay with their mother and learn household skills.

Religions

Not everyone in the Islamic Empire was Muslim. Muslims remained a minority until the tenth century. Even after that date there were still very large communities of Christians, Jews, and Zoroastrians in many places. Zoroastrianism is a religion founded in Persia (modern-day Iran) in the sixth century B.C.E.

Mosques

Mosques were the center of religious life. They were also the center of daily life. Mosques were used as meeting places, schools, and places of worship.

Muslims believe in praying five times each day. The minaret (tower) allows holy men to "call people" to pray at certain times.

بازن وبجبه و دا ع کردو در نیشابور رفت مدتی آنجا کسب کرد هیلفی

Merchants and craftspeople of the empire were legendary for their abilities to bargain for the best prices of goods.

Business

Craftspeople and merchants often worked together. Craftspeople made jewelry, rugs, clothing, pottery, and metal goods. Merchants then sold or traded these items. Craftspeople worked in the back of a shop. The front of the shop was used as a store for their products. Laws protected customers to ensure quality and fair prices.

Caravans

Caravans were important. Goods produced in one area of the Islamic Empire were traded for goods produced in another area. Fifty or more camels crossed large land areas carrying products to trade. It sometimes took months for the caravans to reach destinations.

Shopping in Baghdad was a good way to see how organized business was in the empire. The marketplace was spread of over several acres, but it was easy to find what you wanted. By law, shops with similar products all had to be in the same area. This helped customers find what they needed. Shops next to each other competed for buyers. This made prices lower.

Farming

Muslim farmers grew lots of crops even though the land was dry. They knew how to grow barley and wheat. These crops needed little rainfall. For other crops, special waterwheels lifted water to canals. The canals then transported the water to the fields. Farmers also used advanced methods to fertilize crops and to breed better types of sheep and horses.

In many parts of the Islamic Empire farmers took advantage of year-round warm weather to grow more than one crop on the same land.

You've got mail

The large size of the empire made communication difficult. Carrier pigeons and horses carried official mail. Business people sent their letters with other merchants and traders. To do this the traders had to trust each other. The army also used fires to send light signals.

Chapter 3: Time for Fun

Most entertainment took place at home. Female **Muslims** were not supposed to be seen in public very often. So instead of going out, families played games at home. They also sang or told stories. Reciting poetry was an important form of entertainment. It is still popular in Islamic cultures today.

Many types of people were part of the Islamic Empire. The rulers showed respect for the beliefs of the people they conquered. Muslims celebrated some Christian holidays. It helped the groups live together peacefully.

The city of Jerusalem appears in the background. It is a sacred city to Jews, Christians, and Muslims.

Islamic religious holidays were popular. Ramadan lasts for a month. Muslims show loyalty to God by not eating or drinking certain drinks during daylight hours. At the end of Ramadan Muslims give gifts to the poor.

Muhammad's birthday was another special holiday. The night before his birthday, there was a torchlight parade. On his birthday, leaders made speeches and there were feasts. Many types of entertainers amused the crowds.

Muslims enjoyed celebrations. They held many during the year. They liked to celebrate weddings and births. They also celebrated when children did well in school. Music, dancing, and feasts were common activities. They also liked fireworks displays, games, and storytelling. They enjoyed magic shows and acrobatics.

Parties

Wealthy people had elaborate entertainment in the empire's cities. In Baghdad there are accounts of parties held on boats. The boats were shaped like lions or horses. They were beautifully painted. Musicians and singers performed as guests floated down the river. People decorated colorful costumes with precious jewels.

A birthday is a time for celebration in Muslim nations. This celebration is in the country of Brunei.

By doing the hands-on activities and crafts in this chapter, you'll get a feel for what life was like in the Islamic Empire.

Recipe: Arab Pancakes

One caliph said Baghdad's favorite food was *Katayif*, or Arab pancakes. The caliph even had a poem written about the pancakes. Today they are eaten at Ramadan and for special celebrations. Many of the ingredients, especially flour, would not be exactly like today's products.

Warning!

An adult should always be present when you are using a stove.

Make sure to read all directions before beginning the recipe.

A feast is prepared before a military leader departs for a mission. Many varieties of breads were made in the Islamic Empire.

Supplies and Ingredients

- Pancake mix (if you prefer, you can make your own batter following any recipe you like)
- 2 ½ cups sugar
- 1 ¼ cups water
- 1 tablespoon lemon juice
- 1-2 tablespoons orange-blossom or rose water
- Heavy whipping cream, or mascarpone cheese
- 1 ¼ cup chopped pistachios or almonds (if you have a nut allergy, you can substitute raisins or other dried fruit)
- Vegetable oil
- Skillet or pan

1. Mix the pancake batter and set aside.

2. Combine the sugar, lemon juice, and water in a pot on the stove. Bring to a boil.

3. Let the sugar mixture simmer over low heat for 10 minutes, or until it seems like syrup.

4. Stir in the orange-blossom or rose water and simmer for a few seconds more.

5. Remove the mixture from the stove. Allow the mixture to cool, then place in the refrigerator. This will be your syrup.

6. Lightly grease the skillet.

7. Heat the skillet until very hot, then reduce the heat and keep it at medium.

8. Pour the pancake batter by the tablespoon into the skillet. You will know the pancake is ready to flip when small air holes appear on the top.

9. When the pancakes are done, dip them in the chilled syrup.

10. Arrange the pancakes in one layer on a flat serving dish. Spread with the whipped cream or mascarpone cheese. Sprinkle on the chopped nuts.

Arab Pancakes

Arab pancakes were usually covered with several types of toppings.

Craft: Create a Tughra

Calligraphy was very highly regarded in the Islamic world. In Turkey, calligraphers and illuminators, or illustrators, worked together to create *tughras*. A *tughra* was an official signature used by sultans or emperors. Each emperor had his own mark. These marks followed strict rules. They all consisted of high shafts and two ovals pointing to the left. The names of the ruler, his father, and sometimes his grandfather appeared in the lower center. The word "tughra" is also used to refer to any kind of unusual, elegant way of joining words into shapes. The shapes can be flowers, animals, or buildings. You can create your own *tughra* using your initials.

Warning!
Read all the directions before beginning the project.

Supplies

- Art paper, cut into a 5- or 6-inch square
- Markers or colored pencils
- Fine, black felt-tipped markers
- Pencil and practice paper
- Templates of circles, ovals, or other shapes, about the size of the art paper squares (can be made from posterboard)

Arabic is written from right to left. The artistic letters of its alphabet made some books works of art in themselves.

1. Chose a shape in which to make your initial—oval, circle, or another shape.

2. Trace a shape template onto your practice paper. This shape will frame your design.

3. Write your initials lightly with pencil inside the shape. Try to find a way to make the letters bend and stretch so that they fit the template shape in a pleasing way. For instance, if your initials are "STO," consider the ways in which you might stretch parts of the "S" so it connects or crosses the "T." Or maybe make the "O" bigger than everything else and fit the "S" and "T" inside. (See Picture A)

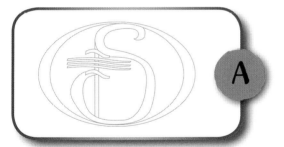

A

4. Think about other people's initials or names that you would also like to include. Maybe you would like to make a design that includes your whole family, or maybe one for you and your friend. Find ways to intertwine these letters with yours.

5. When you think you have the basic design figured out, copy it onto some good art paper. Use the template to make the frame, then lightly sketch in your letter designs.

6. Add floral patterns, animals, architectural elements, geometric patterns, or other decorations to your drawing. What patterns, animals, or other ideas would be good for symbolizing the people this design represents? (See Picture B)

7. When you have drawn in all the details and decorations, outline your designs with a fine-tipped black marker. Use colored pencils or markers to color your design.

8. Learn to draw your basic design with a few flowing, simple strokes.

B

You could use your design to identify your personal belongings or as your signature. For what will you use your tughra?

You may wish to use this design for the next project in the book.

Craft: Decorate a Metal Tray

Craftspeople of the Islamic Empire were famous for making beautiful works of art from metals. Super-heated liquid metals were poured into molds to form basic shapes. After this, metalworkers used a variety of hammers and cutting tools to finish the tray and decorate it. You may wish to use your *tughra* from the previous project as a starting point for this project.

Warning!

This project uses permanent colored markers or paint, be sure to protect your clothing and workspace.

Read all directions before beginning the project.

Supplies

- Disposable aluminum foil baking tray, preferably shallow
- Dull pencils, paint-brush handles, or craft sticks
- Several sheets of paper cut to the size and shape of the bottom of the tray
- Pencils and drawing tools such as rulers, templates, compasses, etc.
- Masking tape
- Soft old dish towel or hand towel, or a softcover student notebook
- Permanent colored markers or permanent paint (optional)

This engraved metal pitcher from Persia dates to 1190 C.E. At this time in Persia most pottery was made of dried clay. The wealthy might decorate such items with metal pieces, but usually did not make an entire pitcher from metal.

1. Take a piece of paper that is the same size as the bottom of your tray. Create a design for your metal tray on the paper. It could be a new form of your *tughra* design, or you could take your inspiration from a geometric pattern, or a pattern of flowers or animals. You may wish to use a repeating pattern of shapes along the edge of the tray. (See Picture A)

A

2. Tape your design to the bottom of your tray. (You may wish to create several options in step one, and try each one out before taping down your final selection.) (See Picture B)

B

3 Place a towel under your tray to make a soft surface. If you do not have a towel, use a folder or notebook that has a paper cover.

4 Use a dull pencil, brush handle, or stick to trace heavily along all the lines on the paper. You have to push hard enough that lines will show on the foil, but do not push all the way through! (See Picture C)

5 Carefully remove the paper. You can touch-up any spots that you missed by pressing directly on the metal with your dull pencil.

6 Consider using markers or paint on your metal design. The markers or paint have to be permanent or they will not stick to the metal.

Decorative Metal Tray

Many of the same decorations on such metal trays are the same as those used 1,000 years ago by craftspeople of the Islamic Empire.

For what will you use the tray? Will your design influence how you use the tray?

Activity: *Pachisi*

Western parts of India, including what is now Pakistan, were once part of the Islamic Empire. *Pachisi* developed in the fourth century in this area. *Pachisi* means 25, a number important in the game. One story says that rulers in the area played the game on life-size boards, using human beings as game pieces. Many cultures around the world had similar "cross and circle" games, so called for the shape of their boards. Today *pachisi* is still played around the world. The directions below are one simplified version of the game.

Warning!

Read all directions before beginning to play.

Supplies
- Pachisi game board, or poster board and markers for creating board
- 2 dice
- 4 game pieces per player, these can be made from construction paper

Numerous board games were popular during the time of the Islamic Empire. Here, two gentlemen show off their chess board.

1 If you are making your own game board, copy the game board pattern in Picture A on to a piece of posterboard. Decorate the board and your pieces however you like. If players in ancient times did not have a game board, they would draw one in the dirt or sand. Their game pieces would sometimes be different colored stones. They would use different objects and methods to substitute for dice.

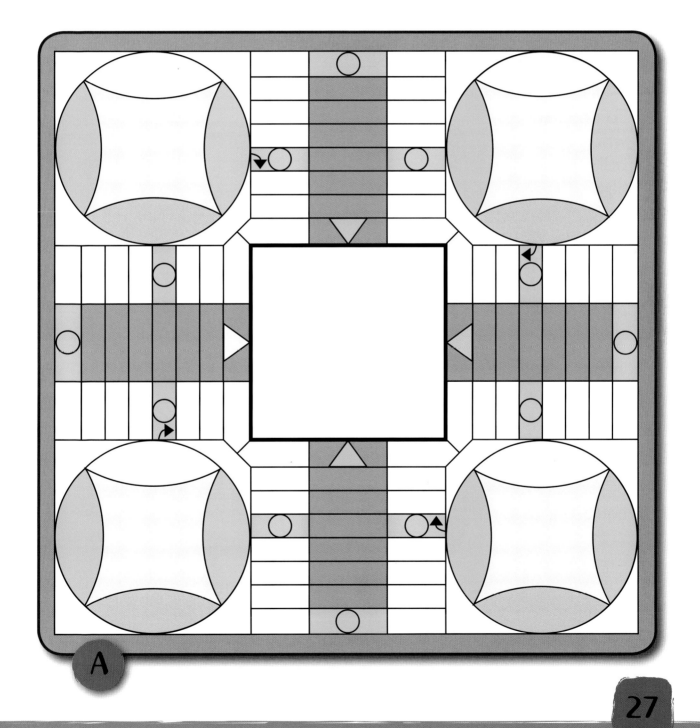

A

2 Place your game pieces in your "base." Notice that each base has two entries on to the game board (See Picture B).

3 To determine who goes first, roll one die. The highest roller starts. The next player should be the person sitting on that player's left.

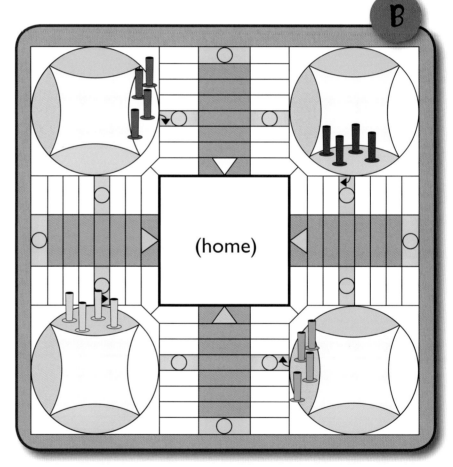

B

(home)

4 To enter a piece into play, roll the dice. You must either roll a five on one of the die, or the total of the dice must equal five (3 and 2, or 4 and 1). Every time you roll a five, you must enter a piece onto the board, until all your pieces are in play. One roll of the dice equals one turn.

❺ For each roll of the dice, you may move one or two of your pieces. For example, if your roll equals six, you may choose to move one piece one square and another piece five squares.

❻ Two pieces may not be on the same space at once. If you land on a square where an opponent is, the opponent's piece is sent back to its "base." (See Picture C)

❼ A piece can only get "home" if you roll the exact count needed to move it into the center square.

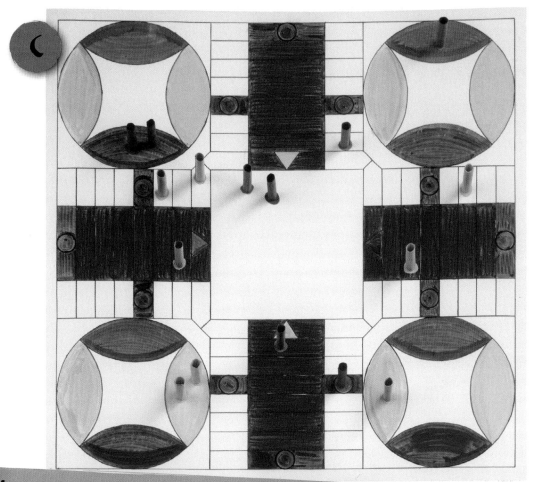

This game is just one variation of a pachisi game. What changes would make the game more exciting or challenging?

Glossary

caravan large group with pack animals, such as camels and donkeys, traveling together

Koran holy book of Islam. Considered by Muslims to be the word of God as revealed to Muhammad.

Middle East region centered in Arabia that extends west into North Africa and east to the eastern border of Iran

Muslim person who follows Islam

More Books To Read

Demi, *Muhammad*. New York: Simon and Schuster, 2003.

Egan, Andrew. *Islam*. Chicago: Raintree, 2003.

Merrill, Yvonne. *Hands on Ancient Peoples, Volume 1*. Salt Lake City: Kits Publishing, 2003.

The instructions for these projects are designed to allow students to work as independently as possible. However, it is always a good idea to make a prototype before assigning any project so that students can see how their own work will look when completed. Prior to introducing these projects, teachers should collect and prepare the materials and be ready for any modifications that may be necessary. Participating in the project-making process will help teachers understand the directions and be ready to assist students with difficult steps. Teachers might also choose to adapt or modify the projects to better suit the needs of an individual student or class. No one knows what levels of achievement students will reach better than their teacher.

While it is preferable for students to work as independently as possible, there is some flexibility in regards to project materials and tools. They can vary according to what is available. For instance, while standard white glue may be most familiar to students, there might be times when a teacher will choose to speed up a project by using a hot glue gun to fasten materials for students. Likewise, while a project may call for leather cord, it is feasible in most instances to substitute vinyl cord or even yarn or rope. Acrylic paint may be recommended because it adheres better to a material like felt or plastic, but other types of paint would be suitable as well. Circles can be drawn with a compass, or simply by tracing a cup, roll of tape, or other circular object. Allowing students a broad spectrum of creativity and opportunities to problem-solve within the parameters of a given project will encourage their critical thinking skills most fully.

Each project contains an italicized question somewhere in the directions. These questions are meant to be thought-provoking and promote discussion while students work on the project.

Index